The Good Wine
Served Last

The Good Wine Served Last

THOMAS HANRAHAN

Library of Congress Control Number:		2012915645
ISBN:	Hardcover	978-1-4797-0582-5
	Softcover	978-1-4797-0581-8
	Ebook	978-1-4797-0583-2

This book was printed in the United States of America.

To order additional copies of this book, contact:
Xlibris Corporation
0-800-644-6988
www.xlibrispublishing.co.uk
Orders@xlibrispublishing.co.uk
304818

Contents

Troubled Beginings

Coming Home

Troubled Beginings

Troubled Beginings

Finding, searching, troubled beginnings.
Where does 'He' lead me ? So concerned.
Vessel unworthy of the treasure, so elusive.
Yet within one's reach so promised.

Little hands and feet eager, anxious to serve.
So unworthy of the prize. Being challenged,
being sincere. Is there a thread holding me
back ? Why am I troubled ? What do I fear ?
Sincerity forthcoming leads me there.

Schizoid With Hope

Stumbling, fumbling, wide awake.
Searching, hiding, still I wait.
Into the battle, din of drums.
Eyes glancing. Dare I go ?
Hymn of praise on my lips.
Forward marching, no retreat.
Heavy burdened, stained but bright.
Looking back has no foresight.
See the summit, fraying rope, grimy
hands, hold out with hope.

Mirror Image

A

I faced the mirror Lord inspired.
It really was revealing.
My image of "Him" genie not, warm caresses, forgiving,
Chiding, smiling. Streams of Love, foibles, cracks,
vanity fair. Intellect pride, self deception, straining, striving.
Take your time. Convert in drops. Don't try to understand.
Take "His" hand, feeble step. He cautions, understands.

B

Restricted Thought

Through thickened glass caged view.
Perceiving things, objects, creatures near and far.
Unable to communicate clearly, bound in isolation den.
"Restricted Thought" Sometimes seeing, feeling dimly
freedom of moving thought.
Restricted mostly in isolated pain, chained to body,
torn in restricting strain.
Pray release, freedom from this frame.
Is God and man oblivious to this plight ?
Surely not, all are caught in this Apocalyptic night.

Without Full Hearts Desire

Morbid state, no embryo of true action.
No spark of Loves desire.
On pyre, in mire of self accusing state.
Ego stripping time descends once more.
On floor. Who accuses you ? Who can see ?
Only "YOU LORD" me on knee in fleeing state.
Lord, is there only I in state of transitory blight ?
Such a sight, envy, pride, greed, consolation need,
Without Full Hearts Desire.

Hostel Living

Adrift, home wood, washed inevitably
upon hostel shores. Wife, children, family,
in present distant past. Fellow sufferers
huddle together, mixed lot, in different
states of limbo.

Some in transit, others stationary, motionless,
in restless alertness, awaiting deliverance,
freedom to take control of lost bye gone
days, dimly remembered, nostalgic tear, well
hidden, suppressed shattered dreams, now
stigmatised.

Prescribed medication, impatience born of
frustration, heavily tested, sedated. Hands
unprepared, sloppy meals unseasoned with
loving care. Compulsive eating, fingers
greasy, clothes ill fitting to behold.

Silent communication erupts with
proscribed liquid medication consumed by
one beside herself with dwindling hope.
There is a presence here, a presence to
the naked stark reality of humanities
apparent abandoned blight.

Amid all this there is fellowship, true
fellowship, shared and unshared. No warm
pictures, knick knacks adorn the place,
supervision, fire proof doors and
windows, furniture required.

Hostel cold inside looking out. Who looks
in ? Occupants sensitive, some holding on
to remnants of pride, dignity denied them,
not by choice. Enter friendly community
nurse, family own to care, all alert, ill at
ease, prisoners of destiny trying to appease,

∕ℒℬ

Brittle Iron Man

*Serrated edge cuts deep, flesh impregnated with
steel. Bone marrow erupts forth, drenched in blood.
Clotted time, brittle fire, no's no mercy.
Purging fire, light coloured skin, Ego dancing,
elopes in dread.
Dreaded iron, cuts so deep. Soldier cries in agony.
White flag raised, pistol spent, maimed, drained,
Surrendered Brittle Iron Man*

Holy Thursday, Thomas, Peter, Thee

❧

Holy Thursday, Thomas, Peter, Thee
In Gethsemene, olive garden green, scene serene ?
Surely not, "He" cried out even now today.
Pray pass this cup, accepted will for Thee.
Peter thrice denied "Him" How many times have we ?
Thomas, Peter, now we amongst them, eager bitter tears
do fall. Resurrection proof to Thomas, Peter's remorse,
drawn forth from cross, weakness, frustration, sin, "He"
did feel about that dreadful din.
Is Thomas, Peter's proof remorse, now required of Thee ?
Tonight, today, early morn,, drinking dens, rollicking away.
Two thousand years seem changed not. O Lord, that awful
din. So few, nay none, you nor I awake, Apostles too they
slept. Lord forgive, have mercy, take cup from me, if it be
your will.

ß

Mystical Response

Awake at last. All is passed, in solitude once more. Time to work, to pray, to think, to escape. No eyes can see, No ears can hear, Life's totality score.

Negativity tugs at sleeve, dampened by human hearts desire. No mire, no fire, "Alert" conscious of "His" presence once more.

What are opportunities ? Lost if merely seen as profit and gain, weighing the Soul in pain, strain.. Strive not, the Kingdom obtained, must reign, supreme, serene.

For who are you and I but dust and ashes moulded in a dream. The ground is firm, now it's soft, bite on bit, bridle tug, five furlongs out to sea.

Caution thrown to the wind, opens shoals of darting fish to control. Still waters run deep. Why !!!Shoulders crouched in defence are but mere buffer zones. Stand erect when needed. Unicorn Love. Lion Pride, squabble at table of desire.

Ego Eye

The Ego that is I, cannot see clearly the why.
It dances, prances, like a peacock unable,
to spy the eye.
The Eye is all seeing, surrounded in Light.
In spite of it's brightness, I am drawn to the centre, unable
to shutter mine Eyes.

Reach Out

Unlocked, not quite, isolated, self conscious moments.
Give, Receive, Empty. Trapped? Fearful? Angry?
anxious moments? Make the journey, search,
brotherhood, sisterhood, unite.

No straining, carve your name on the Tree of Life.
Hesitate, wait, anticipated action not possible.
Partake in Eucharistic Meal. Join the Vine, cast off
deception, admit, reflect, reflect, repent, "REACH OUT"

Time to fly

&

Flight must make, in the wake
of lessons life supporting learned,
received.

Whenever space encroaches space,
like as in mirrored creature life,
the spider work, its weaves of cosy
thread, a bed of no escape it makes.

Escape the tangled life about, look,
take flight, freedom,growth, pay
heed, natures way, webs of life
do ensnare, pay attention, yes,
time to fly needs mention.

B

Staggered Dreams

Stag, refined, elegant, lanky, munches ferns.
Oh so plenty. Alert nearby, mountain lion, poised cat crouches.

Senses betwixt between, scene serene.

Creatures all, man and beast rush nearby to catch the feast.
Hunter, hunted, cloudless skies, girl boy, enjoy Teddy Bear
Picnic.

Nearby streams of nature will pursue.
Lord, all is bright, what a sight.

Natures way more in tune, with ebb and flow
of Life's contradictions.

Too, too far away, man, woman, at play. Knowledged
children, God's free gift, swiftly pass our way.

Stay, listen, do not flee, infinite space, do not dismay. Talk of the
day, Credit Cards, DVD's, Computer Games, Mobile Phones.

The Lords energy deplored. What is the cost of "HIS" Extravaganza of Love ? Dissipated, corrupted, brutalised, destroyed, not yet. Intelligence transmitted from screen to screen, relies on strain, "HIS" pain.

Time for harvest, listen to the cry, if not for "HIM" the girl, the boy, the shy.

Pangs of birth Mother Mary strained, consolation drained, maimed, emptied, little by little, drop by drop. Tears nil to console, Gethsemene pain, preparation gain, Resurrection.

Lord deceive you not, deception galore, pursue gently, hastily open store. Take these lambs of the street, flocking, thronging, about your feet.

Stag must bolt, bob cat too. Grant us peace.
Stop this race. Help us give up chase.
Teddy picnics our surprise.
Forgive us lot, Deceitful Smiles.

B

September Global Thoughts

September beckons patience, Autumn leaves
yet to fall. Snow clad mountains in the distance,
junior/seniors back to school. Somewhere elsewhere
itinerant journeys throughout the night, kindling firewood
being collected.

Crisp cold mornings, blue faced children, school bags new,
surely hoping not yet flu.

Private buses, special buses, city speed, city greed. Bus
inspector, computer fares, none is free.

One step easy, too refined, inclined to slumber, squirrels gather
nuts. Somewhere elsewhere bushfires blazing equator
touched, lamp fires dimming, mushy snow, broken ice,
furry creature blends.

Meanwhile Westward bound wise men follow Star of David Flame. Infant Giant, heavy mantled, will share, draw breath with oxen, sheep and goat.
Snowflakes missing, cows, sheep, goat, will share in Giant Christmas Infant fare.

Jeanne D'Arc

Erect she stood, no orphan.
Knowing from whence she came.

No blame, no shame attributable upon her frame.
Fire brand torches lit, coven gathered to ignite
to death, the accuser of their cruel souls.

Animal passionate men and women will crucify with fire
the subject of their ire, they gathered around Joan their
legions scourge.

Mad they cry, a lie contrived to justify.

Not so, bewitched by Christ, Heavenly King.
Jesus Father, bring to us Justice in our day,
Joan awake, at pray, at rest today.

Mother Mary will unknowingly gently crush with heel
those greedy heads
of serpents so intent on innocent prey.

I give to you allegiance in my crucible of hope.
Give us **bread, bread, bread.**

Coming Home

Presence

Suddenly with jerking motion,
Heavy swelling seas, toss me about
in an ocean of bliss stark awareness,
obliterating action. Spurn my desire.
all is without meaning, unless in 'Him'

Measured peace descends, brief but welcome.
Speed up less you fall into snares of self made
deceit.

Coming Home

With dawning gradual awareness footprints
become visible to me.

Footprints, footprints, mine and mine alone.
My fit, my shape, my depth, my prints.

My path must take, my journey must make.
This journey long ago began, now rediscovered,
begun once more.

(There is a Coming Home in This)

Expanded rooms of my Soul stand erect,
take breadth once more.

Cracks silently trace appear upon the walls.
Awaited, awaited, light peeps through,
there is a familiar :~

(Coming Home in This)
In coming home my heart and Soul combine
in a motion fluid gel mix, gathering, sifting,
attracting, connecting, a cell to cell rebuilding,
a rejoining, a refining, a self to self acquainting,
a renewal taking place.

(There is a Coming Home in This)

Enlightened Thought

Concerned not worried, nervous not anxious. Human feelings acquainted with every man.

Keep the appointments, cancel if necessary.

Strive not too intensely for peace among men

Mercy like peace, drops from Heaven
on those who with reverence and
respect, hold their tongue in anticipation of enlightened thought.

The Fall

Tripped by inquisitive, tempting, forbidden longings.
Triggered by desires of nature. Humanity was
plunged into a torrent of desire.

Innocence split thus between, Eve accused,
Adam guilty. Both in sorrow to deep to measure.

Hive of Angel's Gold

Rejected light, image fright, 'MARY' in the
womb. Womb awoken, JESUS, new born
Adam dawns in honey comb so blue.

'Mary' laboured, received no favours earthly
meant. Heavens opened, new Word spoken
docile donkey sent. Outpoured Word,
flesh adorned, Incense, Mir and Gold.
Age unfolding, thorns upholding, in
'Hive of Angel's Gold'.

Yesterdays Face

There is a calm today compared, all is quite serene.
The storm is over time to dream.

Streams of released tension unfolded, then yesterday,
now in past unloaded. Time to wait relax, refrain,
no fuss, chore ill done, now humdrum.

Beaten drum surrendered once more. By the shore,
lapping waters gently wake thoughts of yesterdays
face, mad dash chase. Today is ours.
May this moment build upon the next.
Gently does it, face to face.

No sudden movements, dwell in gentle place,
no race, just a trace of yesterdays engaged face.
Nay not forgotten, there is a place upon time
capitulated to self imposed race.

Lord, thank you for this pause today, this gift,
yesterday no more, erased. Take me softly gently
to the shore.

Autumn Sight

*Like a child, gushing erupting with excitement, I saw,
danced, leapt, tasted 'Him' dimly. Unobtrusive, not
visible, but yet visible, among the trees, the air, the breeze.*

*The dried empty leaves of Autumn, gently left their
host, in silent transition from life to death to life
again. Colours blend with Season vision, sound, smell,
like a carousel, around and around, the swell in order,
ointment Autumn leaves.*

Mother earth will renew.

*Amid the hedges, grass, trees, there are no humming bees,
chestnuts found in secret hidden place.*

*Season surrenders, obeys the hushed ordered voice.
Ripe Earth ever surrenders, in motion the ocean,
moon sun stars in place.*

Mother 'Mary' blankets, Mothers us from too much sight. Dust and ashes, pearl inside, birth, growth, death, the final ending never written.

Lord, thank you for the gift of sight, delight to see natures way, to play in tune always with final plan, the man, Our God, Jesus Christ in sight.

Lamb in Silence

Amid the trees, mountain top,
shrubbery green, serene, birds in call, insect
flight about cup of tea and me.

With gradual dawning silence, tears of
gratitude, Mother Mary beckoned me.

Sandwich bliss, kiss of tea, so easy there to
say 'I Love Thee' Emptied is mind of useless
thought, full though with fruitful useful
nesting thoughts.

Prepare now nests like this, carefully, for
droplets of spirit growth, growth demands
furrowed soil, surrendered to the plough.
Thank you Mother, cradle me once more,
lamb in silent store.

Mother Mary, bells ring out, crucified yet,
man in ignorance more.

Take us lambs I implore to safety upon shore.

Empty Sandals

He has left us empty sandals.
Unbuckled Soul, toe marks heavily imprinted on leather.

Those sandals worn to vespers, matins,
supper. Silent reminders of life past, they
lie, right and left, empty of energy.

Is he above at Heavens gate, knocking
still, or beyond the many veils and tears
of laughter and woe here below.

Are the cleansing fires through refining
this Soul. Empty questions, empty
sandals, dream no more.

High Appeal

Solomon, nerve of steel, sat upon the bench,
Two women, infant brought him, He in judgement sat.
Impatient plea's, one in terror, considered he the Verdict.
Head upraised, Appeals considered, Porters summoned sent.
Knife at ready, steady, steady, hushed company.
Mother screams, 'No' 'No' 'No' other left unsteady.
No costs awarded, ill afforded, Mother clutches baby.
Woman thief left in grief, shamed not blamed, in Court
of Supreme Appeal.

Noelle

8

You made your entry into this World wrapped
in Christmas tinsel.
Your ways, our ways, chestnuts, walks, the way you
nudged me quiet.
Through you I met other children, Kingdom friends
of my Soul.
I saw you skip, I saw you dance, I saw you laugh
and cry,
But always in my minds eye, I saw a special gift.
Those warmed filled days remembered so, when out
and about, your company to enjoy.
I retrace days sometimes drinking coke, kicking leaves,
carving trees, that secret chestnut place, the tree that
bears our names.
These memories raise my spirits high, squirrels gather
nuts, why cannot I memories store, happy days
explored once more.
How can I say thank you ?
I tasted happiness galore those days, now safe
in memory store.

B

Tame Those Horses

The Fairground carousel around, it goes. Laughter, whirling
happy noises, fill the air, lifeless horse rides, painted fixed
smiles thereon.

No human movement in flesh and blood, no thought of
yesterday today tomorrow, no change, the same it streams,
it echoes endless play.

Those painted carousel horses, mirror seems one's own rigid
trip of mind control.
Thoughts they gallop, no stirrup, no hold on, in equal carousel
horse control, yesterday today tomorrow, no change.

Those horses, their smiling painted faces, fairground
carousel din, laughter, fun. Compared a carousel of created
horses, to thoughtless human mind control.

Around, around, you must get off, to rest, to see,
to hear the grounded reality. The carousel created,
weary nowhere goes, it plants not shoots to life enrich,
fleeting happiness it streams.

Carousel horses smile hauntingly. Energy never expended,
no movement in flesh and blood, no thought, no heart,
the carousel mindless blind control.

Those wide opened eyed carousel horses, sleep not, bright
eyes dazzling, candy floss, human thought sometimes
compares to this.

Let go the reins, pray silence, listen, listen,
the carousel mind control is our illusory pursuit.
Swallow this lesson, be content, to stare sometimes,
saying nothing, difficult this.

Take those horses, break them, tame them, stroke them still.
Be gentle with them, there yours and mine, we know them
well in our minds control.

Let us tame those horses.

&

Holy Innocents (Beslan, Russia) 2004

The Lambs of Beslan have passed, dispatched away.
School days first, school bags new, pencils, copies,
there in love to view.
Ironed shirts, the boys, dresses bright, the girls.
Parents proud, their lunches neatly packed with love.
There in Beslan a silent vacant turmoil gap,
that awful happening left.
No children laugh, no cry, no goodbye kiss, no play,
violence had its way that day.
Those Innocent Lambs, their voices, their laughter,
no more heard.
Memories painfully burn, scorch, scar, brand their
parents minds, hearts, and Souls.
Surely no rest from pain so raw, a crucifying grief
pervades that place.
Those Lambs no judgment theirs to hold, to keep,
no right, no wrong, no discernment vision, just vessels
in wholly opened trust.

That happening, the how, or why, just crumbles, fades
away, begs a massive balm.
Mothers, Fathers, Brothers, Sisters, theirs a public
witnessed grief.
Innocence slain, laid to rest.
Cold clay? A grave ?
A plot of upturned soil?
Those Innocent Lambs of God have attained Eternal rest.

A Finite Beat

The heart of flesh beats silently.
Hidden, exposed not to gaze of life nor light.

Its constant working beat, strong or weak,
it drums, sustains, a silent tribute celebration
of life in transit, in motion.

Yet a finite march must make, a finite struggle,
a final beat awaits. In time an awesome silence
fills it's place, no more, it's journey finite, ends.

Imagine revealed, if ears could hear, the thundering
beating hidden hearts of all. Those states of fear,
happiness, sadness, anguish, loss, engraved thereon,
the crumpled muffled final beat of life departing
empty gone.

Surely a human equality state would be laid
naked level bare above that fragile beating din.

The heart of man/woman immeasurably deep.
Those skirmishes, those joys, those sorrows of heart,
recorded, upheld, supported by a hidden rhythmic
ebb and flow within.

That working beat of flesh, that heart within us all,
inevitably an utter awesome finite silence call.

Celebrate the gift of life, its Springtime moments glow,
stand erect believe this Garden Eden Earth, a temporary
transit place, a place of learning must.

B

Once An Open Blacksmiths Place

No more the common sight of yester year, the blacksmiths place. No bellows puff,
no clanking anvil, no noise of metal hammer met, no horse stood still, no sudden hissing
sound of red hot metal water dipped, no horseshoes handmade, cooled to shape,
no longer common view, the metal softened hammered bent, pierced for holding nails,
the horse, the shoes, the fit, the task.

No more the common sight, the dark filled open door, there to gawk within.
No more the working pair, man and beast, the art, the craft, the skill, therein
partners, joined in common need. Those curious childrens eyes no more, no longer
peer to see, to hear what seemed a magic task complete, a horse stood still,
a blacksmiths noisy gentle work, the horse, the shoes, the fit.

No more to see that leathered apron man, the blacksmith
by the forge, a horse
in stillness wait, submissive stance, the beast with man, the
man with beast,
side by side, a horse awaits shoes of measured fit, beside a
forge with roaring
embers glow, a blacksmiths basic tools to hand.

Once An Open Blacksmiths Place.

Retiring Outlook, Weather View

The sails now trimmed, a smaller boat decked out. The helm,
charts, sextant,
instruments old remembered, not now in view.

Invisible longitude latitude lines target trace life's
unchartered course. No familiar
hands on deck, harbour empty seems, questions, provisions
will they last? Will
natures boat surrounds hold firm in weather fair or foul?
Lifted anchor, untied
ropes, nostalgic fettered lines now severed.

A new horizon slowly shapes, blending, melting, a present
beginning unfolds.
Uneasy step for some, waters seem so deep.
Life's experience holds sway, adjusting course, steady helm,
new
adventure, old sea legs builds confidence on deck.

Fresh winds blow, the certain call of byegone days seems to yell "Steady as she goes" You take hold, release the past, the helm is yours once more.

Retiring Outlook, Weather View

Elaine, At Home Alone, I See

꩜

I will always see, as I see, my "Little Pony One"
that's Elaine, impish, honest, innocent at play.
Rough and tumble she, get it sorted stuff, but free.
She is here, she is there, her name recorded, etched,
firmly written, a forever lively authentic Soul.
She scrawled her name, acquired her rightful place in life.
Her mark boldly distinctly imprinted on the Book of Life.
Is she perfect ? Who is ? She is not !!!
But who can love Perfected Beings in this Life.
A statue, an icon, a Diva, a pot of saved up lolly.
There is a crack in everything. That's how the light gets in.
My Elaine is real, her core, I clearly see her heart.
In flesh and bones she flusters, blusters, brightens up the place.
In school she was an imp at heart, always rough and tumble
fun alive.
She played some pranks, report cards I signed for her with glee.
Now she is a woman a husband children own to care.
Yet I will always love her childish impish way, her heart I see.
Her schoolbook always ill prepared, impatient, untidy she.

Yet she played the game of life for broke, her loving heart an open book, spending is for fun, she strutted out her stuff, held back nothing in reserve. The nut brown hair those impish sparkling eyes. She is, was, still, will forever more be my Elaine, my imperfect perfect love "My Forever Little Pony Queen"

One Summer Picnic Day Remembered

I remember a bright dazzling sun warmed day.
A silent still, a bliss encounter gently penetrated,
reigned supreme abundant love upon my Soul,

In an instant moment, the very essence of my Soul
awoke in a joyful coming home awakening.

In hushed filled silence, a single humming distant
sound, a droning insect flight about the silence broke.
It witnessed, intent it seemed, not to disturb scene
serene, Eden Garden touched.

Did God "His" finger touch that day ?
Did nature combine, conspire, obey, "His" voice command. ?
A surrendered peace descended, enveloped us both.

No utterances, we sat back to back.
"He" surely must have smiled?
A gentle victory moment, a happening,
an event, encounter steeped in honest open love.

In the still of one precious moment.
One Summer Picnic Day, Remembered Forever.

Caterpillar—to—Butterfly

&

Butterfly, butterfly, bright coloured wings
graceful flights does in Summer bring.

Caterpillar, caterpillar, creature slow,
will transform, renew, rebirth, to go.

'Where will you go ?
'Why will you go ?

Recalled memories none, Heretofore in witness
an inaudible feeding frenzied life scene

Crunch, crunch, crunch, munch, munch, munch,.
food, food, food, scenery greenery, gobble
gobble gobble.

Caterpillar, caterpillar, always food in need, indeed, yet
never greed.

Butterfly, butterfly, will you remember ?
Will you recall this your Caterpillar life
gone past ?

Will you creep, crawl away, hide for, seek for
some Resurrection Day ?

Will you die ? Will you then fly ?

In modesty will you curl up in a self-made
changing room ?

A tomb ? A womb of sorts ?
Surely must the Creator have planed design.

Behold a life change puzzle this ? Why ?

'Butterfly' can, will you reveal, confide your reasoned
journey tale?

The why, the where, the heretofore begin.

You will change clothes, you will lose
weight, wings you will procure. ?

Is this some inbuilt self made magic plan ?
Will God Creator continue, retouch with hand
"His" plan.

With foresight, did you see a beauty feast,
your beauty heart desired, to dine in, to wine
in, to join in, some sunny Summer day.

Butterfly ways, sways in fragile Swan Lake
ballet dance. Maybe one, maybe two. No more
than three or four, signals Summer warmth
in store, flower top visits in command.

Flights with lightweight wafer flutter motions,
dancing, standing still, in trance at times.

Butterfly flower proposals, bridal gowns,
bridal suites, gentle splendid colours blend,
creation to creation, delicate wafer thin
encounter tends.

Meanwhile a catwalk called, therein we
human forms, our beauty clothes display no end,
whilst Butterfly conforms to simple 'Master
Plan' natures hand to hand.

Pause, stay, stand, gaze awhile at one of natures
total silent stock, freedom dance, no hurry, no
worry, in truth, their life is brief, fleeting,
fleeting, so close, so close to curtain call,
unaware bliss.

Multicoloured adorned, theirs an almost scented
form, shapely wafer thin design, natures
programmed butterfly, caterpillar linked.

Butterfly, Butterfly my thinking speaking Soul
awakes, believes in a "Resurrection Life"
caterpillar to butterfly compared in flesh
exampled.

Human stock arise take note Resurrection Life is
promised thus. A newly spirit formed
spendour body ours a 'Resurrection Life' transformed be.

A mirrored caterpillar to butterfly spirit body
frame, yet unending, an eternal resurrection
gain.

Thereafter human hopes and dreams, must expect
an equal resurrection life, a Butterfly eternal
refrain.

No not the same, no, not the same, believe,
anticipate, celebrate, unending, unending. Toil,
concern, worry, dreams, hopes, consigned, transmuted,
a harmony, a unity, an ever lasting
present past combined, a consummated realised
love transcending bliss, forever, forever, truly promised
granted.

"Moladgh Go Deo le Dia"

Destiny Pause

Destiny sometimes places life on pause.
We are challenged with that call.

Will I ponder a step begin?
Realize a dream begun before ?

Can you see the path.?
Do you believe?
Do you dare to trust ?
Do you see an open faithful heart ?
Do you dare to reach, to touch ?

The how, or why, no matter much.
Always, therein, a reasoned lesson purpose.
The Season Spring suggests, offers beginnings,
an end to Season Winter's Destiny Pause,
answers always, it will bring.

Imbued with patience, emerge from Winter's paused
retreat, renewed,
drenched in hope,
ripe to reach, to greet again, shoots of
growth anew.

Herein therein a dream, a hope revealed.
To harvest life, a dream must form within a living root,
begin it's natural growth,
fruit within without will grow.

Surrendered to the soil of life, sincerity leads these words,
these hopes,
these seeds of Love, longed for, prayed for, yet to be realized.

Remember, Destiny sometimes holds Life
on pause, therein invites, permits, consents
belief in a future Season's Harvest crop.

B

My Twin Soul

There is a sheltered garden spot within my Soul.

Therein an indoor eye, reveals a bridge flower adorned,
a colour scent invites but one, you alone can view this
hidden secret place.

Moonlight prances, dances, enchantment, magic secret spells.
Tonight human Souls partake in midnight dance.

They bathe beneath the Moon, away from prying eyes,
content, joyful, unaware of things about. Nearby moonlit
pools of water gently glistens trickles patient love between
the pebble stones.

In morn the dew, it's hazes sun uplifts. Noon heralds butterfly
encounters, their silent flutter dance will enhance enchant
this secret place. Sound, birds in call, bright plumage and
a song. From tops of trees, vantage points on high, the
feathered species invites his mate the two unison harmony
will complete.

Complete my garden Soul, wall, or fence, to hold our dream within. My love, your fragrance warmth, your outward inward smile, your presence real and full. A simple touch, a golden thread connects.

Fruit of the vine, we sip together, we two alone, our eyes Are full to brim, in a naked love embrace.

Angels sing, dance, issue magic spells and potions. Love confetti scattered in the air, about our feet, an extravaganza protected Fairyland of Dreams. All this and more, your fashioned sculpted body female frame, its slender curves dovetails with mine, like a glove upon my fingered being.

Harmony thaws ice, the Winter grip, my Soul unlocks, my every sense, awakes takes hold, my heart becomes a cosy fire aglow, its warmth, its touch, its depth, its everything and more.

Surely, truly, Heaven plays an active part in this, guiding prompting, seeking out, a tailor fit, threads of harmony will complete.

B

Silent Moment

Alone we are one, at silence, therein an awesome wonderful
innocent depth, a pure
love, a Universe, a hidden
Pearl of wealth, the riches of our Souls, we plummet merge,
enjoy.
Relaxed at peace natures way settings, distant distractions,
noises, fade, give
way to simply bliss.

Pray Soul to Soul, man and woman Blessed.
Listen gently, trickling water, a babbling brook across soft
pebble stones rush
between our toes, our toes, they dangle happily, side by
side, they touch,
caress and say hello.

With love glazed eyes, hearts at rest, we glance, believe,
with hearts transparent
core, our beings communicate, no words, honestly, openly,
trustingly, lovingly secure.

Freedom love is given thus, shared, accepted,
no conditions pertain.

This is I, this is She combined, an experience forever
recorded, encounterd, a
Heavenly Spirit Kiss, a private secret hidden "Love Coelesce".

Mine Eyes Do See

On that day, Heaven sent, when behold,
I will see once more the glory of your person. Revealed
your figure standing full in front of me, your eyes, your
hair, your female body form will speak to me in
volumes.

Without a word, you will balm my spirit Soul, you will
touch my inner eye with joy.

I will weep with joyful rejoicing on that day. Why !! Maybe
warm tears flowing freely will you see, open full surrender
may you witness, naked, exposed, trustfully embraced
against your Soul.

Blackberry Picking In The Sky

Blackberry, strawberry, apple pie, amber hazes in
the sky. Bernadette busy, Brain in shed, joinery,
refinery, wholemeal bread. Custard mustard, ham delicious
who pray tell washes dishes. Paul in slumber hair fair meant,
minds not he, who pays the rent. Derek pensive, easy
cool, eye on table playing pool. School days beckon, Tom
asleep, sheep a herding, meadows bleep. Morning dawning
he a lying, raises up sleepy head. Rip Van Winkle in a
Tinkle, now, Theresa Kate enthralled, Siobhan too there,
wide awake. Bernadette busy making cake. Rhubarb Tart and
Apple Pie, Blackberry Picking In The Sky.

Scent of Love

Ponder thus a "Lady Sweet" a Scent of Love.
This flower, my flower, my love to be,
in thoughts, by hour, by hour.

A threshold view, a coming home anew.
I trust, she soon will be with me.

With hands outstretched, an open door, a thirst,
a hunger feel, it lingers so upon my being.

No earthly food, drink, company, can fill this gap,
my open house in view, this flower, my flower, my heart
upon a second minute hourly beat, it waits.

The marrow of my bones, long to feel, to touch,
to gently mingle with her Soul.

No touch, no sight, no sound, no earthly presence can
compare, a spirit wake,
a spirit blessed, a gentle stirring pulse of light within
confirms my Soul, a path to take.
My Soul, a moment pause connection bliss.

A lip to lip encounter seal, a Holy kiss confirms this.
My Heart upon an open Winter fire writes these
words and feels the comfort heat.

By my side, soon my blanket other half will come home,
my dream,
this flower, this scent of Brother, Sister, lover, my
Hearts desire.

My Heart, My Soul, My Mind

If I could choose my Soul a place to rest.
Sunshine days I'd forever view with her.
If life permitted a merely fleeting Love embrace,
to hold you briefly, memory flash frames this picture
on my mind.

Her honey sweet kiss, forever imprinted on my lips,
my heart, My Soul, my mind, will always certain
hold this photo frame.

Why!! My memory already holds a picture feast,
Her golden hair, her slender body frame, her all embracing
smile, her stand by me,
her hand supporting, lovingly, loyally, strong, Her strength,
Her substance,
Her honest, kind, and gentle ways.

Lightning Source UK Ltd.
Milton Keynes UK
UKOW041130140613

212255UK00005B/32/P